# Yell and Scream for Your Team!

Tracy Kompelien

Consulting Editor, Diane Craig, M.A./Reading Specialist

**ABDO**
Publishing Company

Published by ABDO Publishing Company, 4940 Viking Drive, Edina, Minnesota 55435.
Copyright © 2007 by Abdo Consulting Group, Inc. International copyrights reserved in all countries.
No part of this book may be reproduced in any form without written permission from the publisher.
SandCastle™ is a trademark and logo of ABDO Publishing Company.

Printed in the United States.

Credits
Edited by: Pam Price
Curriculum Coordinator: Nancy Tuminelly
Cover and Interior Design and Production: Mighty Media
Photo Credits: Shutterstock, Steve Wewerka

Library of Congress Cataloging-in-Publication Data
Kompelien, Tracy, 1975-
  Yell and scream for your team! / Tracy Kompelien.
      p. cm. -- (Synonyms)
  ISBN-13: 978-1-59928-733-1
  ISBN-10: 1-59928-733-1
  1. English language--Synonyms and antonyms--Juvenile literature. I. Title.

PE1591.K658 2007
421.8--dc22
                          2006031423

SandCastle™ books are created by a professional team of educators, reading specialists, and content developers around five essential components—phonemic awareness, phonics, vocabulary, text comprehension, and fluency—to assist young readers as they develop reading skills and strategies and increase their general knowledge. All books are written, reviewed, and leveled for guided reading, early reading intervention, and Accelerated Reader® programs for use in shared, guided, and independent reading and writing activities to support a balanced approach to literacy instruction.

## Let Us Know

SandCastle would like to hear your stories about reading this book. What is your favorite page? Was there something hard that you needed help with? Share the ups and downs of learning to read. We want to hear from you! To get posted on the ABDO Publishing Company Web site, send us e-mail at:

**sandcastle@abdopublishing.com**

**SandCastle Level: Fluent**

A synonym is a word that has the same or a similar meaning as another word.

Here is a good way to remember what a synonym is:

**synonym**
**=**
**same**
**=**
**similar**

3

# synonyms

When we play soccer,
there are many rules.

laws

regulations

policies

# synonyms

The crowd likes to yell
for their team.

roar

shout

scream

howl

cheer

# synonyms

Our coach, Mr. King, teaches us the game.

pastime

sport

activity

12

# synonyms

Madison is a quick runner.

speedy

fast

rapid

swift

brisk

14

# synonyms

Sam warms up before the swim meet. Sam trained a long time. Today he swims for five minutes. Sam prepares for his meet.

Can you find any synonyms for the phrase warms up in the paragraph above?

15

16

# synonyms

The fans roar when their team scores a goal. The fans cheer and clap. They jump and shout when they are excited. There are many fans at the game.

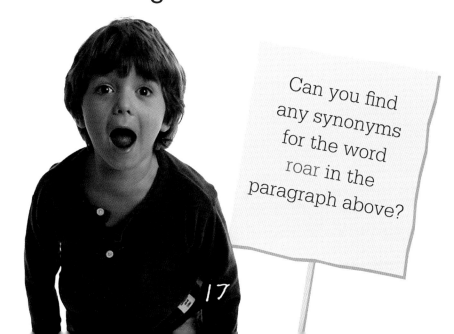

Can you find any synonyms for the word roar in the paragraph above?

17

18

# synonyms

Kate takes a brisk walk. She also likes to run. When she runs, she is fast. And when she walks, she is a speedy walker.

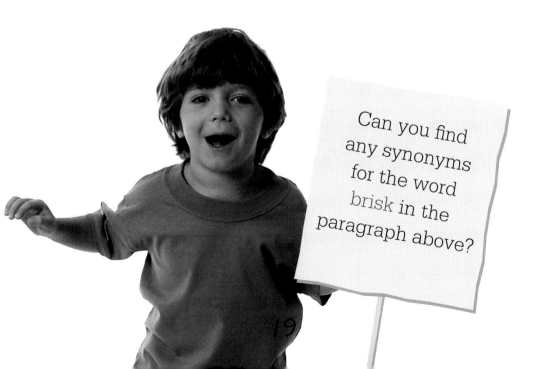

Can you find any synonyms for the word brisk in the paragraph above?

19

What synonyms can you use to describe the crowd's cheers?

# Glossary

**goal** – points scored for getting a ball or puck into a specific area during a game.

**pastime** – an enjoyable activity done in one's spare time.

**policy** – a plan for guiding how things will be done.

**regulation** – a rule or order.

**train** – to prepare for something by learning and practicing.

# Words I Know

## Nouns

A noun is a person, place, or thing.

activity, 9

coach, 9

crowd, 7, 20

fans, 17

game, 9, 11, 17

goal, 17

laws, 5

meet, 15

minutes, 15

pastime, 9

policies, 5

regulations, 5

rules, 5

runner, 13

soccer, 5

sport, 9

swim meet, 15

synonyms, 20

team, 7, 17

time, 15

walk, 19

walker, 19

## Proper Nouns

A proper noun is the name of a person, place, or thing.

Kate, 19

Kyle, 11

Madison, 13

Mr. King, 9

Sam, 15

# Words I Know

## Verbs
A verb is an action or being word.

are, 5, 17
can, 20
cheer(s), 7, 17, 20
clap, 17
describe, 20
howl, 7
is, 13, 19
jump, 17
likes, 7, 11, 19

play, 5
practice, 11
prepare, 11, 15
rehearse, 11
roar, 7, 17
run, 19
scores, 17
scream, 7
shout, 7, 17

swims, 15
takes, 19
teaches, 9
train, 11, 15
use, 20
walks, 19
warm up, 11, 15
yell, 7

## Adjectives
An adjective describes something.

brisk, 13, 19
excited, 17
fast, 13, 19
five, 15
his, 15

long, 15
many, 5, 17
our, 9
quick, 13
rapid, 13

speedy, 13, 19
swift, 13
their, 7, 17
what, 20

# About SandCastle™

A professional team of educators, reading specialists, and content developers created the SandCastle™ series to support young readers as they develop reading skills and strategies and increase their general knowledge. The SandCastle™ series has four levels that correspond to early literacy development in young children. The levels are provided to help teachers and parents select the appropriate books for young readers.

**Emerging Readers**
(no flags)

**Beginning Readers**
(1 flag)

**Transitional Readers**
(2 flags)

**Fluent Readers**
(3 flags)

These levels are meant only as a guide. All levels are subject to change.

To see a complete list of SandCastle™ books and other nonfiction titles from ABDO Publishing Company, visit www.abdopublishing.com or contact us at: 4940 Viking Drive, Edina, Minnesota 55435 • 1-800-800-1312 • fax: 1-952-831-1632